CW00519262

THE BRITISH LIBRARY

DIARY 2005

MEDIEVAL LIFE

FRANCES LINCOLN

Frances Lincoln Limited
4 Torriano Mews
Torriano Avenue
London NW5 2RZ
www.franceslincoln.com

The British Library Diary 2005
Published in association with The British Library, London
Copyright © Frances Lincoln Limited 2004
All illustrations copyright © The British Library Board 2004
All text copyright © The British Library Board 2004

Astronomical information reproduced, with permission,
from data supplied by HM Nautical Almanac Office, copyright
© Council for the Central Laboratory of the Research Councils.

All rights reserved. No part of this publication may be
reproduced, stored in a retrieval system or transmitted, in any
form, or by any means, electronic, mechanical, photocopying,
recording or otherwise, without either prior permission in
writing from the publishers or a licence permitting restricted
copying. In the United Kingdom such licences are issued by the
Copyright Licensing Agency, 90 Tottenham Court Road,
London W1T 4LP

British Library cataloguing-in-publication data
A catalogue record for this book is available from
The British Library

ISBN 0-7112-2349-1
Printed in China

First Frances Lincoln edition 2004

FRONT COVER: *A scene from the 'Roman de la Rose'. Bruges, c.1490–1500. Harley MS 4425, f.12.*

BACK COVER: *A lover addressing three ladies. Bruges, c.1490–1500. Royal MS 16 F.ii, f.188.*

TITLE PAGE: *A border from a fifteenth-century French book of hours. Add. MS 27697, f.200v.*

ABOVE: *An aspiring fiddle-player, from a Flemish book of hours, c.1300. Stowe MS 17, f.145v.*

OVERLEAF, LEFT: *A landscape in Flanders. Detail of an illumination from 'Le Trésor des Histoires'. Bruges, c.1470–1480. Cotton MS Augustus A V, f.345v.*

CALENDAR 2005

JANUARY	FEBRUARY	MARCH	APRIL
M T W T F S S	M T W T F S S	M T W T F S S	M T W T F S S
1 2	1 2 3 4 5 6	1 2 3 4 5 6	1 2 3
3 4 5 6 7 8 9	7 8 9 10 11 12 13	7 8 9 10 11 12 13	4 5 6 7 8 9 10
10 11 12 13 14 15 16	14 15 16 17 18 19 20	14 15 16 17 18 19 20	11 12 13 14 15 16 17
17 18 19 20 21 22 23	21 22 23 24 25 26 27	21 22 23 24 25 26 27	18 19 20 21 22 23 24
24 25 26 27 28 29 30	28	28 29 30 31	25 26 27 28 29 30
31			

MAY	JUNE	JULY	AUGUST
M T W T F S S	M T W T F S S	M T W T F S S	M T W T F S S
1	1 2 3 4 5	1 2 3	1 2 3 4 5 6 7
2 3 4 5 6 7 8	6 7 8 9 10 11 12	4 5 6 7 8 9 10	8 9 10 11 12 13 14
9 10 11 12 13 14 15	13 14 15 16 17 18 19	11 12 13 14 15 16 17	15 16 17 18 19 20 21
16 17 18 19 20 21 22	20 21 22 23 24 25 26	18 19 20 21 22 23 24	22 23 24 25 26 27 28
23 24 25 26 27 28 29	27 28 29 30	25 26 27 28 29 30 31	29 30 31
30 31			

SEPTEMBER	OCTOBER	NOVEMBER	DECEMBER
M T W T F S S	M T W T F S S	M T W T F S S	M T W T F S S
1 2 3 4	1 2	1 2 3 4 5 6	1 2 3 4
5 6 7 8 9 10 11	3 4 5 6 7 8 9	7 8 9 10 11 12 13	5 6 7 8 9 10 11
12 13 14 15 16 17 18	10 11 12 13 14 15 16	14 15 16 17 18 19 20	12 13 14 15 16 17 18
19 20 21 22 23 24 25	17 18 19 20 21 22 23	21 22 23 24 25 26 27	19 20 21 22 23 24 25
26 27 28 29 30	24 25 26 27 28 29 30	28 29 30	26 27 28 29 30 31
	31		

CALENDAR 2006

JANUARY	FEBRUARY	MARCH	APRIL
M T W T F S S	M T W T F S S	M T W T F S S	M T W T F S S
1	1 2 3 4 5	1 2 3 4 5	1 2
2 3 4 5 6 7 8	6 7 8 9 10 11 12	6 7 8 9 10 11 12	3 4 5 6 7 8 9
9 10 11 12 13 14 15	13 14 15 16 17 18 19	13 14 15 16 17 18 19	10 11 12 13 14 15 16
16 17 18 19 20 21 22	20 21 22 23 24 25 26	20 21 22 23 24 25 26	17 18 19 20 21 22 23
23 24 25 26 27 28 29	27 28	27 28 29 30 31	24 25 26 27 28 29 30
30 31			

MAY	JUNE	JULY	AUGUST
M T W T F S S	M T W T F S S	M T W T F S S	M T W T F S S
1 2 3 4 5 6 7	1 2 3 4	1 2	1 2 3 4 5 6
8 9 10 11 12 13 14	5 6 7 8 9 10 11	3 4 5 6 7 8 9	7 8 9 10 11 12 13
15 16 17 18 19 20 21	12 13 14 15 16 17 18	10 11 12 13 14 15 16	14 15 16 17 18 19 20
22 23 24 25 26 27 28	19 20 21 22 23 24 25	17 18 19 20 21 22 23	21 22 23 24 25 26 27
29 30 31	26 27 28 29 30	24 25 26 27 28 29 30	28 29 30 31
		31	

SEPTEMBER	OCTOBER	NOVEMBER	DECEMBER
M T W T F S S	M T W T F S S	M T W T F S S	M T W T F S S
1 2 3	1	1 2 3 4 5	1 2 3
4 5 6 7 8 9 10	2 3 4 5 6 7 8	6 7 8 9 10 11 12	4 5 6 7 8 9 10
11 12 13 14 15 16 17	9 10 11 12 13 14 15	13 14 15 16 17 18 19	11 12 13 14 15 16 17
18 19 20 21 22 23 24	16 17 18 19 20 21 22	20 21 22 23 24 25 26	18 19 20 21 22 23 24
25 26 27 28 29 30	23 24 25 26 27 28 29	27 28 29 30	25 26 27 28 29 30 31
	30 31		

MEDIEVAL LIFE
SCENES FROM ILLUMINATED MANUSCRIPTS

The British Library has one of the finest collections of illuminated manuscripts in the world. The selection of images in this diary is an introduction to some of the Library's treasures and to the history of manuscript illumination in the West – one of the most vibrant sources of medieval art. From sheep-shearing to hawking, from courtly love to jousting tournaments and from feasting to music-making we are afforded a glimpse of daily life – in town and country, at work and play and from cradle to grave.

The term 'manuscript' comes from the Latin for 'handwritten': before the invention of printing all books had to be written out by hand. This was a time-consuming and labour-intensive process, and could take months or years, depending on how elaborate they were and how many people were involved. Although paper was used in southern Europe from the twelfth century, it did not become widespread until the late Middle Ages – there was no paper mill in England until the fifteenth century – and before this the usual material for writing on was parchment or vellum, made from stretched, treated animal skins. A large manuscript might take one whole cow- or sheep-skin to make a folded sheet of two to four pages, and a thick book could require the hides of entire herds. Medieval books were therefore expensive items, and book-ownership was not the casual affair it is today.

Some manuscripts were made even more precious by 'illumination'. This term comes from the Latin word for 'lit up' or 'enlightened' and refers to the use of bright colours and gold to embellish initial letters or to portray entire scenes. Sometimes these are purely decorative, but often they combine with the text to mark important passages, or to enhance or clarify the meaning.

Around 1200 provision of education shifted from the cathedral schools to universities in European cities such as Paris, Bologna and Oxford. Although some of the monastic scriptoria which had been responsible for book production before continued to function, manufacture was increasingly centred upon the towns. Secular stationers would take commissions from patrons, increasingly many of them students or other lay people, and would sub-contract out work to a variety of specialized craftsmen and women on a piecework basis. New texts began to circulate for the urban and rural secular elite and middle classes, such as works on natural history (the bestiary), the Apocalypse, and the Romance. Books of Hours, geared to private devotion, emerged as the most popular book and the vernacular languages grew ever more frequent alongside Latin. Increasingly, scenes illustrating medieval life adorned the manuscript page, with visual evocations of milieux as diverse as biblical history and the court of King Arthur being embroidered with details drawn from contemporary life.

DR MICHELLE P. BROWN
Curator of Illuminated Manuscripts
The British Library

DECEMBER 2004 • JANUARY 2005

---

27 MONDAY
Holiday, UK, Republic of Ireland, Canada
Australia and New Zealand (Christmas Day observed)

---

28 TUESDAY
Holiday, UK, Republic of Ireland, Canada
Australia and New Zealand (Boxing Day observed)

---

29 WEDNESDAY

---

30 THURSDAY

---

31 FRIDAY
New Year's Eve
Holiday, USA (New Year's Day observed)

---

1 SATURDAY
New Year's Day

---

2 SUNDAY

Garlanded dancers emerging from the gates of Constantinople, beneath trumpets adorned with banners of the Luttrell and Sutton families. Detail from the Luttrell Psalter. England, c.1325–1335. Add. MS 42130, f.164v.

3 MONDAY

Holiday, UK, Republic of Ireland, Canada
Australia and New Zealand
Last Quarter

4 TUESDAY

Holiday, Scotland and New Zealand

5 WEDNESDAY

6 THURSDAY

Epiphany

7 FRIDAY

8 SATURDAY

9 SUNDAY

Chopping wood for the fire. A calendar page for January from the 'Golf Book', a Flemish book of hours illuminated by Simon Bening, c.1540. Add. MS 24098. f.18v.

JANUARY

10 MONDAY
New Moon

11 TUESDAY

12 WEDNESDAY

13 THURSDAY

14 FRIDAY

15 SATURDAY

16 SUNDAY

A translator at work in his study, from 'Le Livre de Valerius Maximus', made in Bruges for King Edward IV, 1479. Royal MS 18 E.iii, f.24.

17 MONDAY
Holiday, USA (Martin Luther King's birthday)
First Quarter

18 TUESDAY

19 WEDNESDAY

20 THURSDAY

21 FRIDAY

22 SATURDAY

23 SUNDAY

Scenes in a counting-house. Genoa, late fourteenth century. Add. MS 27695, f.8.

JANUARY

24 MONDAY

25 TUESDAY
Full Moon

26 WEDNESDAY
Holiday, Australia (Australia Day)

27 THURSDAY

28 FRIDAY

29 SATURDAY

30 SUNDAY

An apothecary's shop. The apothecary (to the right) is prescribing a cure to a customer. He will mix ingredients from the jars on his shelves. French, early fourteenth century. Sloane MS 1977, f.49v.

31 MONDAY

1 TUESDAY

2 WEDNESDAY
Last Quarter

3 THURSDAY

4 FRIDAY

5 SATURDAY

6 SUNDAY
Holiday, New Zealand (Waitangi Day)

Birds gather around Bartholomaeus Anglicus, the author of 'De proprietatibus rerum', and some falconers. Bruges, 1482. Royal MS 15 E.iii, f.11.

FEBRUARY

7 MONDAY

8 TUESDAY

Shrove Tuesday
New Moon

9 WEDNESDAY

Ash Wednesday
Chinese New Year

10 THURSDAY

Islamic New Year (subject to sighting of the moon)

11 FRIDAY

Holiday, USA (Lincoln's birthday)

12 SATURDAY

13 SUNDAY

Amazon women riding to war, from a chronicle of world history made in the Crusader Kingdom of Jerusalem. Acre, c.1286.
Add. MS 15268, f.123.

. de homine siue de muliere .
experimenta .

BRITISH MUSEUM

14 MONDAY
St Valentine's Day

15 TUESDAY

16 WEDNESDAY
First Quarter

17 THURSDAY

18 FRIDAY

19 SATURDAY

20 SUNDAY

Two lovers on a bench, starting to show the effects of an aphrodisiac potion. From a manuscript Herbal. Lombardy, c.1400. Sloane MS 4016, f.44v.

FEBRUARY

21 MONDAY
Holiday, USA (President's Day)

22 TUESDAY

23 WEDNESDAY

24 THURSDAY
Full Moon

25 FRIDAY

26 SATURDAY

27 SUNDAY

A man called Amram awakes from a dream while his wife sleeps. From the 'Speculum Historiale' by Vincent of Beauvais, made in Bruges for King Edward IV, c.1480. Royal MS 14 E.i, vol 1, f.77.

28 MONDAY

1 TUESDAY
St David's Day

2 WEDNESDAY

3 THURSDAY
Last Quarter

4 FRIDAY

5 SATURDAY

6 SUNDAY
Mothering Sunday, UK

A public execution; Amerigot Marcel is about to be beheaded. From Froissart's 'Chronicles'. Bruges, c.1472. Harley MS 4379, f.64.

MARCH

7 MONDAY

8 TUESDAY

9 WEDNESDAY

10 THURSDAY

New Moon

11 FRIDAY

12 SATURDAY

13 SUNDAY

Setting out for a day of hawking, from a fifteenth-century French book of hours. Add. MS 31834, f.6.

... ... michi. ... ...

bar voluntatem.

Ne derelinquas me domine de

us meus ne discesseris a me.

Intende in adiutorium meum

domine deus salutis mee.

14 MONDAY
Commonwealth Day

---

15 TUESDAY

---

16 WEDNESDAY

---

17 THURSDAY
St Patrick's Day
Holiday, Northern Ireland and Republic of Ireland
First Quarter

---

18 FRIDAY

---

19 SATURDAY

---

20 SUNDAY
Palm Sunday
Vernal Equinox

Nuns sitting in choir stalls, from the so-called Psalter of Henry VI. France, c.1420. Cotton MS Domitian A.xvii, f.73v.

MARCH

21 MONDAY

22 TUESDAY

23 WEDNESDAY

24 THURSDAY
Maundy Thursday

25 FRIDAY
Good Friday
Holiday, UK, Republic of Ireland, Canada,
USA, Australia and New Zealand
Full Moon

26 SATURDAY

27 SUNDAY
Easter Day
British Summertime begins

A mill-house in Flanders, with the miller at his window. Detail of an illumination from 'Le Trésor des Histoires', c.1470– 1480.
Cotton MS Augustus A V, f.345v.

GRA·PREVENIES

GRA GRATV·FACIE

GRA·GRATIS
DATE

Leupositeur.

28 MONDAY

Easter Monday
Holiday, UK (exc. Scotland), Republic of Ireland,
Canada, Australia and New Zealand

29 TUESDAY

30 WEDNESDAY

31 THURSDAY

1 FRIDAY

2 SATURDAY

Last Quarter

3 SUNDAY

Three 'Graces', representing virtues, stand by a fountain which contains the lilies of France and the roses of England. A scene from a French book of pageants intended for the marriage of Mary Tudor to King Louis XII of France, 1514. Cotton MS Vespasian B.ii, f.6.

APRIL

4 MONDAY

5 TUESDAY

6 WEDNESDAY

7 THURSDAY

8 FRIDAY
New Moon

9 SATURDAY

10 SUNDAY

Horses at work in the fields – harrowing (in the foreground) and ploughing. A calendar page for April from the 'Golf Book', a Flemish book of hours illuminated by Simon Bening, c.1540. Add. MS 24098, f.26v.

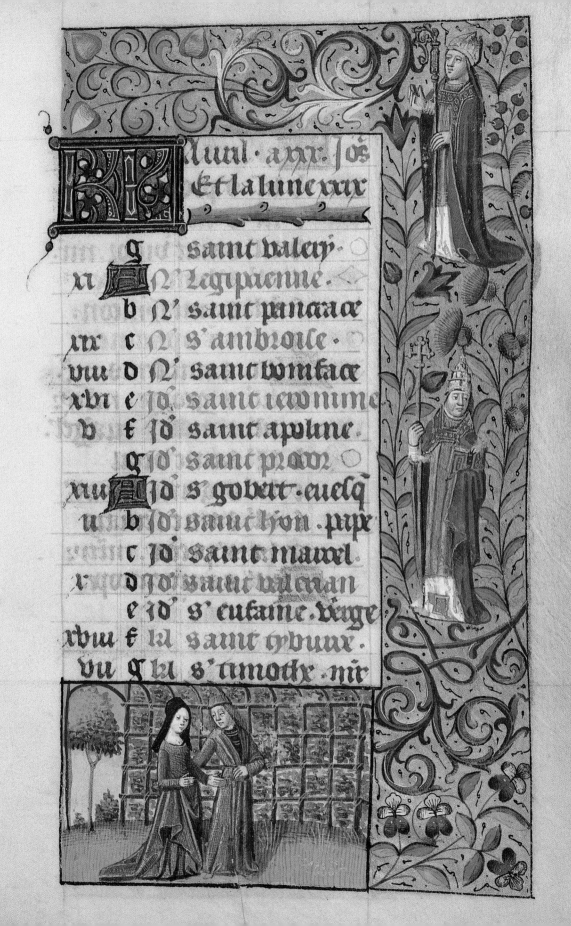

KL

uil · xxx · ioſ
Et la lune xxix

g		saint valery
xi	N'	legiptienne
b	N'	saint pancrace
xix	c	N'	s'ambroiſe ·
viii	d	N'	saint boniface
xvi	e	id	saint ieronime
v	f	id	saint apoline ·
g	id	saint prior
xiii	A	id	s'gobert · evelq
ii	b	id	saint lyon · pape
c	id	saint maxel
x	d	id	saint valerian
e	id	s'eufame · verge
xviii	f	kl	saint trouux ·
vii	g	kl	s'timothe · mir

11 MONDAY

12 TUESDAY

13 WEDNESDAY

14 THURSDAY

15 FRIDAY

16 SATURDAY
First Quarter

17 SUNDAY

A calendar page for April, from a late fifteenth-century French book of hours. Add. MS 4836, f.4.

APRIL

18 MONDAY

19 TUESDAY

20 WEDNESDAY

21 THURSDAY
Birthday of Queen Elizabeth II

22 FRIDAY

23 SATURDAY
St George's Day

24 SUNDAY
Passover (Pesach), First Day
Full Moon

Making a fence around a house. The man in the foreground strips the willow. Bruges, c.1480. Add. MS 19720, f.288v.

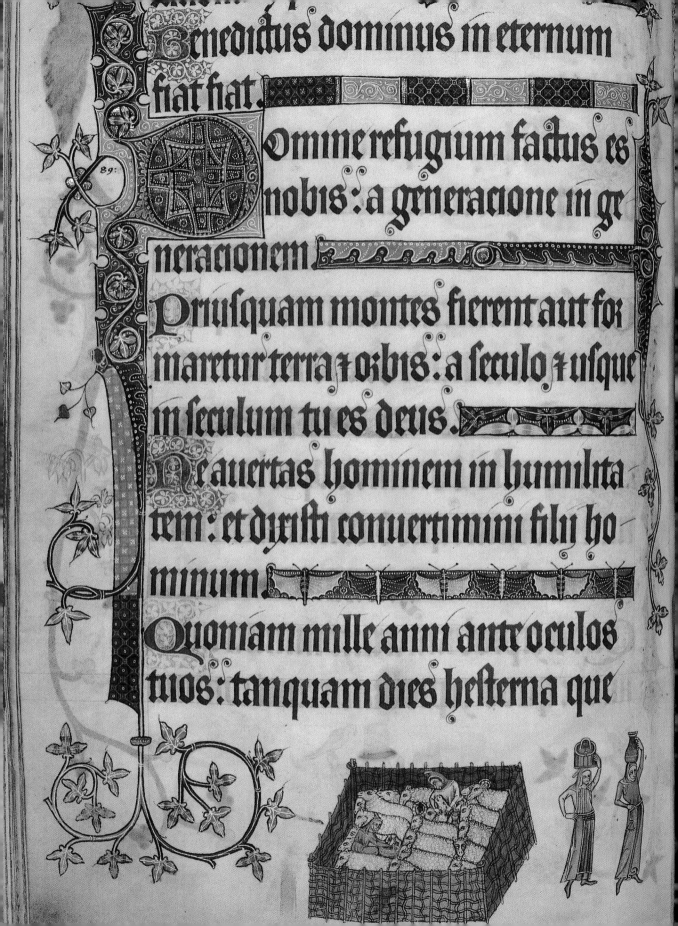

Benedictus dominus in eternum fiat fiat.

Omine refugium factus es nobis: a generacione in generacionem

Priusquam montes fierent aut formaretur terra ꝫ orbis: a seculo ꝫ usque in seculum tu es deus.

Ne auertas hominem in humilitatem: et dixisti conuertimini filii hominum

Quoniam mille anni ante oculos tuos: tanquam dies hesterna que

25 MONDAY

Holiday, Australia and New Zealand (Anzac Day)

26 TUESDAY

27 WEDNESDAY

28 THURSDAY

29 FRIDAY

30 SATURDAY

Passover (Pesach), Seventh Day

1 SUNDAY

Passover (Pesach), Eighth Day
Last Quarter

Sheep are in their sheep-pen to be milked and the milk is being carried away by the two people on the right. From the Luttrell Psalter. England, c.1325–1335. Add. MS 42130, f.163v.

MAY

2 MONDAY
Early May Bank Holiday, UK and Republic of Ireland

3 TUESDAY

4 WEDNESDAY

5 THURSDAY
Ascension Day

6 FRIDAY

7 SATURDAY

8 SUNDAY
Mother's Day, Canada, USA, Australia and New Zealand
New Moon

Two ladies present a prize to the winner of a jousting tournament. From the 'Romance of Perceforest'. Flanders, late fifteenth century. Royal MS 19 E.ii, f.129v.

9 MONDAY

10 TUESDAY

11 WEDNESDAY

12 THURSDAY

13 FRIDAY

14 SATURDAY

15 SUNDAY
Whit Sunday (Pentecost)

Primitive people enjoying an idyllic outdoor life. From the 'Roman de la Rose'. Bruges, c.1490–1500. Harley MS 4425, f.76v.

MAY

16 MONDAY
First Quarter

17 TUESDAY

18 WEDNESDAY

19 THURSDAY

20 FRIDAY

21 SATURDAY

22 SUNDAY
Trinity Sunday

Nature shows Vaillance (the lady in the tent) to the author in a dream. From Jean de Courcy, 'Chemin de Vaillance'. Bruges, late 1470s. Royal MS 14 E.ii, f.i.

Et quant le iour fut be
m oye la messe et dictes ses
heures de besuigner ie nel ces
si Et tant que a laide de dieu
ou roy et de madame il fut
darmes de destriers et de
tresriche puement et autel
habillement si bien en point
que bonez durie se quil eust
bn suffist a bug baron royal
Et atant laisseray en...

...nulter de toutes ces choses
et du grant bruit qui par
tout estoit de ces armes et
de la priere que chun faisoit
pour luy qui tant estoit
senne et menu honune au
regart du chevalier voulans
quil sembloit a chascun
que tous les coups le souil
loit Et diray des armes
fites au iour et terme donne

Conuent le seigneur de loisselench z sautrebindret et le...
fant leurs armes a cheval puit le roy la royne z pluseurs
arnces senuieulx z... Baron... ordonne de commencer leurs
armes Le seigneur de loisse...
uant le xxv iour ...lench fist ce matin soubz le
fut venu apres ce ...hourt du roy... xx grant
que fautre eut ...lances toutes armees fort de
ofte lempuise au
seigneur de loisselench z sou

23 MONDAY
Full Moon

24 TUESDAY

25 WEDNESDAY

26 THURSDAY
Corpus Christi

27 FRIDAY

28 SATURDAY

29 SUNDAY

Two knights joust in a tournament, watched by the king and queen of France. Broken lances from previous jousts litter the ground. France, c.1470. Cotton MS Nero D.ix, f.55v.

MAY • JUNE

30 MONDAY
Spring Bank Holiday, UK
Holiday, USA (Memorial Day)
Last Quarter

31 TUESDAY

1 WEDNESDAY

2 THURSDAY

3 FRIDAY

4 SATURDAY

5 SUNDAY

Building a house in the country, from Petrus de Crescentiis, 'Ruralium Co-modorum Libri XII'. Bruges, c.1480. Add. MS 19720, f.27.

6 MONDAY

Holiday, Republic of Ireland
Holiday, New Zealand (The Queen's birthday)
New Moon

7 TUESDAY

8 WEDNESDAY

9 THURSDAY

10 FRIDAY

11 SATURDAY

The Queen's official birthday (subject to confirmation)

12 SUNDAY

A knight and his lady ride to a tournament, from Froissart's 'Chronicles'. Bruges, c.1472–1473. Harley MS 4379, f.99.

JUNE

13 MONDAY
Jewish Feast of Weeks (Shavuot)
Holiday, Australia (The Queen's birthday)

14 TUESDAY

15 WEDNESDAY
First Quarter

16 THURSDAY

17 FRIDAY

18 SATURDAY

19 SUNDAY
Father's Day, UK, Canada and USA

Sheep-shearers at work, a short distance away from a country hostelry. A calendar page for June, illuminated by Simon Bening. Bruges, c.1540–1550. Add. MS 18855, f.109.

20 MONDAY

21 TUESDAY
Summer Solstice

22 WEDNESDAY
Full Moon

23 THURSDAY

24 FRIDAY

25 SATURDAY

26 SUNDAY

In this illustration of Psalm 95, David is introducing his musicians to a 'new song' of angels saluting the birth of Christ. From the Isabella Breviary. Bruges, c.1490–1497. Add. MS 18851, f.164.

JUNE • JULY

27 MONDAY

28 TUESDAY
Last Quarter

29 WEDNESDAY

30 THURSDAY

1 FRIDAY
Holiday, Canada (Canada Day)

2 SATURDAY

3 SUNDAY

Picking cherries off a tree, from a late fourteenth-century North Italian manuscript. Sloane MS 4016, f.30.

Cerasia. sup. arb
ceresia.

4 MONDAY
Holiday, USA (Independence Day)

5 TUESDAY

6 WEDNESDAY
New Moon

7 THURSDAY

8 FRIDAY

9 SATURDAY

10 SUNDAY

A wedding scene, from Valerius Maximus, 'Facta et Dicta Memorabilia'. Possibly Bruges, c.1470. Royal MS 17 F.iv, f.65v.

JULY

11 MONDAY

12 TUESDAY
Holiday, Northern Ireland (Battle of the Boyne)

13 WEDNESDAY

14 THURSDAY
First Quarter

15 FRIDAY
St Swithin's Day

16 SATURDAY

17 SUNDAY

A ship filled with armed men, setting off to conquer the Canary Islands, from 'Le Canarien'. France (Paris), after 1404.
Egerton MS 2709, f.2.

ous oubliez Melencolie
Et pour faire chiere plus lie
Ung doulx matin aux champs yssy
Ou prenmes sour quamours sailie
les vers et la saison jolie
fait cesser ennuy et soucy

18 MONDAY

19 TUESDAY

20 WEDNESDAY

21 THURSDAY
Full Moon

22 FRIDAY

23 SATURDAY

24 SUNDAY

Four ladies are depicted meeting Alain Chartier (the author of this book, 'Le Livre de Quatre Dames') and they tell him about the fate of four knights at the battle of Agincourt, 1415. France, c.1425. Add. MS 21247, f.1.

JULY

25 MONDAY

26 TUESDAY

27 WEDNESDAY

28 THURSDAY
Last Quarter

29 FRIDAY

30 SATURDAY

31 SUNDAY

Hay-makers at work in the fields. A calendar page for July, illuminated by Simon Bening. Bruges, c.1540–1550. Add. MS 18855, f.109v.

AUGUST

1 MONDAY
Summer Bank Holiday, Scotland and Republic of Ireland

2 TUESDAY

3 WEDNESDAY

4 THURSDAY

5 FRIDAY
New Moon

6 SATURDAY

7 SUNDAY

Pilgrims on the road to Canterbury. An illumination by a Flemish artist, c.1525. Royal MS 18 D.ii, f.148.

AUGUST

---

8 MONDAY

---

9 TUESDAY

---

10 WEDNESDAY

---

11 THURSDAY

---

12 FRIDAY

---

13 SATURDAY

First Quarter

---

14 SUNDAY

Men and women reaping corn. From the Luttrell Psalter. England, c.1325–1335. Add. MS 42130, f.172v.

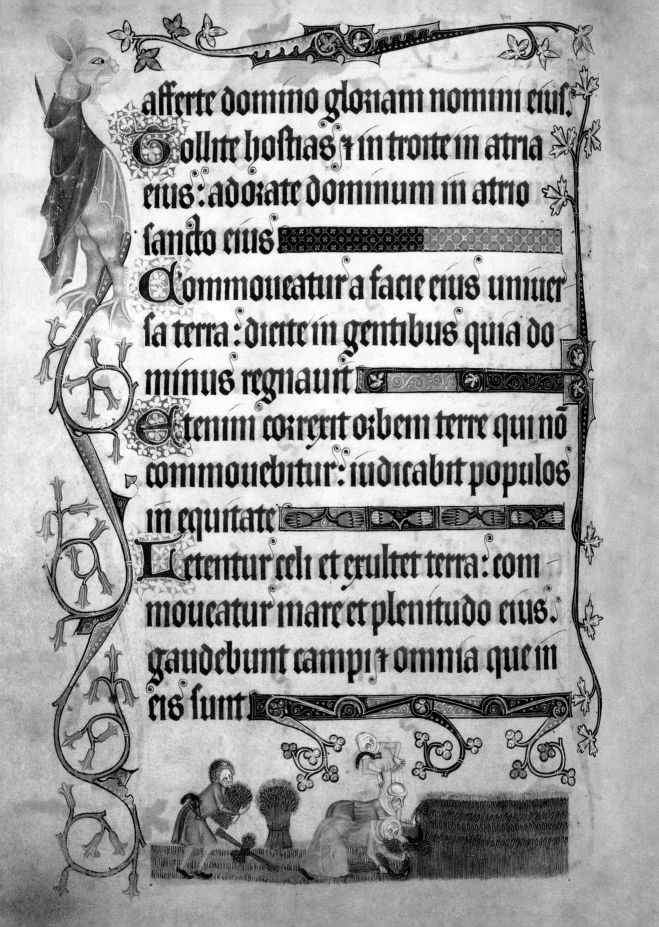

afferte domino gloriam nomini eius.

Tollite hostias ⁊ introite in atria
eius: adorate dominum in atrio
sancto eius

Commoueatur a facie eius uniuer
sa terra: dicite in gentibus quia do
minus regnauit

Etenim correxit orbem terre qui nō
commouebitur: iudicabit populos
in equitate

Letentur celi et exultet terra: com
moueatur mare et plenitudo eius.
gaudebunt campi ⁊ omnia que in
eis sunt

15 MONDAY

16 TUESDAY

17 WEDNESDAY

18 THURSDAY

19 FRIDAY

Full Moon

20 SATURDAY

21 SUNDAY

Knights joust in front of a huge crowd of spectators. A calendar page for August from the 'Golf Book', a Flemish book of hours illuminated by Simon Bening, c.1540. Add. MS 24098, f.23v.

AUGUST

22 MONDAY

23 TUESDAY

24 WEDNESDAY

25 THURSDAY

26 FRIDAY
Last Quarter

27 SATURDAY

28 SUNDAY

A cooper with one of his barrels, and the sign of the zodiac 'Virgo' above him. A calendar page for August from an Italian book of hours, c.1400. Add. MS 34247, f.8.

Augustus ht dies .xxxj. luna uo .xxx.

c Sancti petri aduincula.
d no
c no Inuentio sci stephani.
f no
g no Sca dominica ofcsse.
a id Sca sixti pape 7 m̄.
b id Sca donati epi.
c id
d id Vigilia.
e id Sca laurentij.
f id Scor̄ tiburtij 7 susme.
g id Sce clare uirginis.
a id Cassiani 7 ypoliti.
b kl. Vigilia.

29 MONDAY
Summer Bank Holiday, UK (exc. Scotland)

30 TUESDAY

31 WEDNESDAY

1 THURSDAY

2 FRIDAY

3 SATURDAY
New Moon

4 SUNDAY
Father's Day, Australia and New Zealand

Men boiling brine in a copper bowl, heated by a furnace below. From 'Le Trésor des Histoires', a Flemish manuscript of c.*1470–1480.*
Cotton MS Augustus A.V, f.363.

SEPTEMBER

5 MONDAY
Holiday, Canada (Labour Day) and USA (Labor day)

6 TUESDAY

7 WEDNESDAY

8 THURSDAY

9 FRIDAY

10 SATURDAY

11 SUNDAY
First Quarter

A knight on horseback, the suitor of a princess (depicted overleaf) from a fifteenth-century German allegorical treatise on chess. Add. MS 21458, f.32.

12 MONDAY

13 TUESDAY

14 WEDNESDAY

15 THURSDAY

16 FRIDAY

17 SATURDAY

18 SUNDAY
Full Moon

A princess, seated with a bird in the hand, from a fifteenth-century German allegorical treatise on chess. Add. MS 21458, f.18.

SEPTEMBER

19 MONDAY

20 TUESDAY

21 WEDNESDAY

22 THURSDAY
Autumnal Equinox

23 FRIDAY

24 SATURDAY

25 SUNDAY
Last Quarter

Joseph depicted interpreting the dreams of Pharaoh's butler and baker, from a late fifteenth-century Flemish Bible history.
Add. MS 39657, f.108v.

26 MONDAY

27 TUESDAY

28 WEDNESDAY

29 THURSDAY

Michaelmas Day

30 FRIDAY

1 SATURDAY

2 SUNDAY

Planting vines and harvesting grapes in a vineyard. Bruges, c.1480. Add. MS 19720, f.80.

OCTOBER

---

3 MONDAY

New Moon

---

4 TUESDAY

Jewish New Year (Rosh Hashanah)
First Day of Ramadân (subject to sighting of the moon)

---

5 WEDNESDAY

---

6 THURSDAY

---

7 FRIDAY

---

8 SATURDAY

---

9 SUNDAY

Wine from the new vintage is ready to taste. A calendar page for October from the 'Golf Book', a Flemish book of hours illuminated by Simon Bening, c.1540. Add. MS 24098, f.27v.

Aprés seynt Edward reg
na Harald le fiz Gode
wyn. count de Kent. a fort
e a tort. ix. moys. dunk ve
ent Will' bastard. e ly tol
yst la vye e le regne e qquist
la tete. Harald gist al bail thm.

Puis regna Will' bai
ard xxi. an. puis mo
rust. e gist a Kame en
Nmundye.

10 MONDAY

Holiday, Canada (Thanksgiving Day)
Holiday, USA (Columbus Day)
First Quarter

11 TUESDAY

12 WEDNESDAY

13 THURSDAY

Jewish Day of Atonement (Yom Kippur)

14 FRIDAY

15 SATURDAY

16 SUNDAY

William, Duke of Normandy killing King Harold at the battle of Hastings (1066). England, c.1280–1300.
Cotton MS Vitellius A.xiii, f.3v.

OCTOBER

17 MONDAY
Full Moon

18 TUESDAY
Jewish Festival of Tabernacles (Succoth), First Day

19 WEDNESDAY

20 THURSDAY

21 FRIDAY

22 SATURDAY

23 SUNDAY

A monk-cellarer fills a flagon of wine from a barrel, and takes the opportunity to have a 'tasting' himself whilst he does so. From 'Li Livres dou Sante', a late thirteenth-century French treatise. Sloane MS 2435, f.44v.

24 MONDAY

United Nations Day
Holiday, New Zealand (Labour Day)

25 TUESDAY

Jewish Festival of Tabernacles (Succoth), Eighth day
Last Quarter

26 WEDNESDAY

27 THURSDAY

28 FRIDAY

29 SATURDAY

30 SUNDAY

Holiday, Republic of Ireland
British Summertime ends

King Charles VIII of France, with attendant courtiers and a favourite dog, accepts a copy of the book from its author Pierre Louis de Valton, in a French manuscript of pre-1498. Add. MS 35320, f.3v.

OCTOBER • NOVEMBER

31 MONDAY
Hallowe'en

1 TUESDAY
All Saints' Day

2 WEDNESDAY
New Moon

3 THURSDAY

4 FRIDAY

5 SATURDAY
Guy Fawkes' Day

6 SUNDAY

A lay-sister sits at the fireside with a book, preparing medicine for Tobit, the sick man lying in bed. Bruges, 1470. Royal MS 15 D.I, f.18.

7 MONDAY

8 TUESDAY

9 WEDNESDAY
First Quarter

10 THURSDAY

11 FRIDAY
Holiday, Canada and USA

12 SATURDAY

13 SUNDAY
Remembrance Sunday, UK
Remembrance Day, Canada
Veterans' Day, USA

Rome, fortified and ready to withstand a siege. Italy (Florence) c.1431–1447. Harley MS 1340, f.12.

NOVEMBER

14 MONDAY

15 TUESDAY

16 WEDNESDAY

Full Moon

17 THURSDAY

18 FRIDAY

19 SATURDAY

20 SUNDAY

Robert of Anjou enthroned as King of Naples. Italy, 1335–1340. Royal MS 6 E.ix, f.10v.

21 MONDAY

22 TUESDAY

23 WEDNESDAY
Last Quarter

24 THURSDAY
Holiday, USA (Thanksgiving Day)

25 FRIDAY

26 SATURDAY

27 SUNDAY
Advent Sunday

A doctor lets blood from a patient, with another doctor and a patient waiting in a queue behind. Bruges, 1482. Royal MS 15 E.ii, f.165.

NOVEMBER • DECEMBER

28 MONDAY

29 TUESDAY

30 WEDNESDAY
St Andrew's Day

1 THURSDAY
New Moon

2 FRIDAY

3 SATURDAY

4 SUNDAY

Killing a fatted hog, ready for winter. From a late thirteenth-century French manuscript 'Li Livres dou Sante'. Sloane MS 2435, f.46v.

Psallite felices protecti culmine rose
Purpuree. celo quam dedit ipse deus
Anglicolis. et quam iyt distulit pder tell'
Aduentum rose protinus orta fuit
Cuius et in folus radiantia lilia crescunt
Distinctos flores hic parit vna nidit
Albis et rubeis respersa coloribus Intus
In numero florum micuit rosa rubens
Altior ex iunxit flores sptamine cunctos
Pulchrior hic vir est visa colore prior
Corpora fortificans sic mebra debilia curis
Dulcis odorifera pellit et omne malum
Affert leticia. mor tristia visa repellit
Cunctis est morbis distribuenda dosie
Est rex Henricus bis quartus sanguine clarus
Anglorum virtus purpura rosa micans
Huius se mento studeat qs sudere voti

Et vultu placido dicere rosa vile
A sixtu vuletr hbis assanie dulcs
Omnibus accept' gte et ipse suis
Bella gerit hostes viat na rector i ar'
Sera leone iram sic fugiunt emuli
Est et prasic' constas moderate plenc'
Magnanimus Iust losibus atqz iue
Magnific' dulce larg pietate redundas
Munera pro mentis distribues ōnibus
Singula que refert rose est inesa pte
Cuc nullo claudi carmic tanta potest
Psallite fideles protecti culmine rose
Cuius odoratu tristia cuncta cedunt
Fer eterne deus qui mudi septi gubernas
Cui ex gremio funditur ōne honor
Quesum' vt regat des terra legia videre
Et post hoc sedeat rector i arce dei

Salue radix Iacob   producens genuit Iacob

ramn suprema it alto   domus

Queuica

Salue   felix   Anglia

5 MONDAY

6 TUESDAY

7 WEDNESDAY

8 THURSDAY
First Quarter

9 FRIDAY

10 SATURDAY

11 SUNDAY

A musical allegory celebrating the House of Tudor. Flanders, between 1509 and 1516. Royal MS 11 E.xi, f.2.

DECEMBER

12 MONDAY

13 TUESDAY

14 WEDNESDAY

15 THURSDAY
Full Moon

16 FRIDAY

17 SATURDAY

18 SUNDAY

A group of musicians in procession, from a mid fifteenth-century Flemish manuscript. Add. MS 38122, f.90.

19 MONDAY

20 TUESDAY

21 WEDNESDAY

Winter Solstice

22 THURSDAY

23 FRIDAY

Last Quarter

24 SATURDAY

Christmas Eve

25 SUNDAY

Christmas Day

The Virgin and Child, surrounded by music-playing angels, from the Sforza Hours. Ghent, c.1517–1521. Add. MS 34294, f.177v.

DECEMBER • JANUARY

---

26 MONDAY

Boxing Day (St Stephen's Day)
Jewish Festival of Chanukah, First Day
Holiday, UK, Republic of Ireland, Canada, USA,
Australia and New Zealand (Christmas Day observed)

---

27 TUESDAY

Holiday, UK, Republic of Ireland, Canada, USA,
Australia and New Zealand (Boxing Day observed)

---

28 WEDNESDAY

---

29 THURSDAY

---

30 FRIDAY

---

31 SATURDAY

New Year's Eve
New Moon

---

1 SUNDAY

New Year's Day

The Luttrell family and their guests enjoy a feast, from the Luttrell Psalter. England, c.1325–1335. Add. MS 42130, f.208.

i diebus meis inuocabo

mdederunt me dolores m

ericula inferni inuenerui

lacionem ꝫ dolorem inue

i domini inuocaui

NOTES